God's Affirmations For You

A Book of Encouragement

A 12-week devotional practice

Shirley Giles Davis

God's Affirmations For You

A Book of Encouragement

A 12-week devotional practice

by
Shirley Giles Davis

All Scripture quotations contained in this booklet are from the
NIV (New International Version) of the Bible unless
otherwise specified.

This book is available as an eBook as well as a printed publication.
Check on Amazon.com or with your local bookseller to
place an order.

Ebook and print design by Bree Van Dyke of
BVD Freelance Designs.

Dedication:
To my Annex-University Ministry Core
Groups—Past, Present, and Future
May you know God's great
love and care for you…
always.

Table of Contents

Introduction

God's Affirmations for You: A Book of Encouragement has grown out of more than a decade of intentional, prayerful listening and learning. It seems that when I am studying God's Word, or preparing to teach it, or coaching clients about life purpose, or helping people understand God's unique design and gifting of them, I have noted that oftentimes we don't believe God...we don't trust Him. And our lack of belief and trust seems to be rooted in our unwillingness to embrace God's unconditional, unfailing love toward us and His grace and mercy extended to us. We hear that "God is love," but we somehow do not believe that love extends to us personally. We know we are not to try to "earn" God's love, but it's human nature to want to. We respect God. We may even obey God because we know that's the "right" thing to do, but do we truly believe and embrace and live as if we are fully and completely LOVED?

This booklet is designed to help transform what you believe about God, about His unfailing love for you, His kindness and goodness toward you, His compassion and mercy for you, AND how you see yourself. It is formatted for you to walk through and deeply meditate upon one-day-at-a-time for twelve weeks (even repeated four times a year). Each week starts with a reading, provides a daily verse upon which to meditate, and ends with a prayer for the week and an optional exercise or practice.

Leave this book or your e-reader where you will see it each day. It will only require a few moments of your time, but my hope is that, as you engage daily with powerful, encouraging, exhorting,

Introduction

soul-feeding Scripture, old thought habits will be replaced ever so gently but firmly and lastingly with God's thoughts about you.

This booklet is meant to be a gift of grace. If you don't get to it each day in twelve weeks, just return to it when you are able. Repeat it as many times as you like. God's Word never gets old. Never goes out of style. Is always relevant. Always uplifts.

Be encouraged!

Week One—Child of God

According to an article by the Mayo Clinic, "Only 10 percent or so of the variation in people's reports of happiness can be explained by differences in their circumstances. It appears that the bulk of what determines happiness is due to...**thoughts and behaviors that can be changed**" (emphasis mine).[1]

Paul tells us—from prison, mind you—that he "**learned to be content** whatever the circumstances" (Philippians 4:10-13). He goes on to say that learning contentment is directly connected to finding our strength in God, to changing our focus—from ourselves and our circumstances—and putting it on Christ. The rest of Philippians 4 tells of the byproducts of focus on God and not self: decreased anxiety, decreased anger, decreased frustration, decreased striving.

I don't know about you, but I could use some decreases in my anxieties, anger, frustrations, and striving. Paul tells us that when he has a truthful perspective of who God is and who he, Paul, is, he is able to find his satisfaction and security and peace in God alone. Paul's terribly painful and challenging circumstances did not change. But Paul says again in that same chapter: "I have learned the secret of being content in any and every situation, whether well fed or hungry, whether living in plenty or in want. I can do all this through Him who gives me strength" (Philippians 4:12-13).

We are people who specialize in unhealthy rumination. Dwelling on things that are false, wrong, impure, discouraging, or upsetting

---

[1] Tips for Cultivating Contentment, MayoClinic.com, stress management tab.

results in heightened anxiety and lowered joy. Recent research tells us that instead reflecting on the positives can decrease depression, give us a mood boost, help us problem-solve, and focus us—even disrupting our stress.[2] Paul was alluding to the same and taking it two steps further—to contentment, and rooting it in the Lord.

The prescription in Philippians 4:4-9 is summarized well in The Message translation:

> *Celebrate God all day, every day. I mean, revel in him! Make it as clear as you can to all you meet that you're on their side, working with them and not against them. Help them see that the Master is about to arrive. He could show up any minute!*
>
> *Don't fret or worry. Instead of worrying, pray. Let petitions and praises shape your worries into prayers, letting God know your concerns. Before you know it, a sense of God's wholeness, everything coming together for good, will come and settle you down. It's wonderful what happens when Christ displaces worry at the center of your life.*
>
> *Summing it all up, friends, I'd say you'll do best by filling your minds and meditating on things true, noble, reputable, authentic, compelling, gracious—the best, not the worst; the beautiful, not the ugly; things to praise, not things to curse. Put into practice what you learned from me, what you heard and saw and realized. Do that, and God, who makes everything work together, will work you into his most excellent harmonies.*

Because: "Whatever I have, wherever I am, I can make it through anything in the One who makes me who I am" (v. 13). Paul ends this letter to his friends thusly: "Receive and experience the amazing grace of the Master, Jesus Christ, deep, deep within yourselves" (v. 23).

When we focus on—set our minds and hearts on—healthfully

---

[2] https://greatergood.berkeley.edu/podcasts/item/when_rumination_is_good, September 6, 2022.

ruminate on—what is true, noble, right, pure, lovely, admirable, excellent, and praiseworthy, we are increasingly able to receive and experience that GRACE of God deep within. The following pages contain one or two verses per day for this week. Set aside some time to reflect on and internalize God's words to you.

Day 1
You are God's child—born of God.

<u>John 1:12-13</u> Yet to all who did receive him, to those who believed in his name, he gave the right to become children of God—children born not of natural descent, nor of human decision or a husband's will, but born of God.

<u>1 John 5:19</u> We know that we are children of God...

Day 2
You are a dearly loved child of God.

Ephesians 5:1-2 Follow God's example, therefore, as dearly loved children and walk in the way of love, just as Christ loved us and gave himself up for us as a fragrant offering and sacrifice to God.

Deuteronomy 14:1 You are the children of the Lord your God.

Day 3
You are God's child…showered with His lavish love
and being transformed.

<u>1 John 3:1-2</u> See what great love the Father has lavished on us, that
we should be called children of God! And that is what we are!
Dear friends, now we are children of God, and what we will be has
not yet been made known. But we know that when Christ appears,
we shall be like him, for we shall see him as he is.

Day 4
You are a child of the Living God.

<u>Hosea 1:10</u> …they will be called "children of the living God."

<u>Revelation 21:7</u> Those who are victorious will inherit all this, and I will be their God and they will be my children.

Day 5
You are God's child…linked to all God's
children through Christ.

<u>Galatians 3:26-28</u> So in Christ Jesus you are all children of God through faith, for all of you who were baptized into Christ have clothed yourselves with Christ. There is neither Jew nor Gentile, neither slave nor free, nor is there male and female, for you are all one in Christ Jesus.

Day 6
Take a moment now to say the following verse adaptations aloud.
Insert your name in each blank space. Say it over at least twice.
Savor the thought contained in these words direct from
God to your heart:

I [Name] _____ am the Lord's child, born of Him.
I [Name] _____ am dearly cherished by the Lord, showered
with His lavish love.

Day 7
Week 1 Prayer:

Lord, transform my thoughts, change my behaviors, renovate my tendency to ruminate on things that are wrong and that I cannot change. Help me learn to be content whatever is happening in my life and in the world today. Take away my tendency to worry, relieve my frustrations as I focus on You and who You are. Give me Your supernatural strength to persevere. Create in me a holy resilience.

Disrupt my stress as I choose to celebrate and worship You today. I pause now to remember Your grace and mercy to me, to name aloud those things for which I am grateful in this moment, knowing that detailing my gratitude is how You want me to fix my mind…how You want me to live. *[PAUSE and list at least five things for which you are grateful.]*

I declare that I am awestruck by the fact that You, the God of the universe, call me Your child…Your dearly beloved. I am overwhelmed by Your lavish, limitless love. I find myself grateful that Your love connects me with all others in Your Body (Your Church)—from all peoples, places, and nations. How remarkable!

Highlight that which is true, noble, right, pure, lovely, admirable, excellent, and praiseworthy in and around me. May I know Your GRACE deep in my soul, mind, and spirit today.

I pray all of this by faith in Your precious Name,
Amen.

Optional Week 1 Activity:

If these things upon which you have meditated this week are true of God and of you...how should you then live?

Take a moment to jot down—in a journal, in a "note" on your phone, on a Post-It note that you place where you will see it often—the thing(s) this week's meditations are stirring for you. Simply writing something down can help you process and synthesize your thoughts into something meaningful and deepen your understanding.[3]

---

[3] See https://reflection.ed.ac.uk/reflectors-toolkit/producing-reflections/ways-reflecting/written; The University of Edinburgh.

Week Two—Loved...Unfailingly...by God

In recent years, the Lord has helped me see and know that His LOVE always comes before my calling and purpose...before my actions and service. For myself and for many, we can give intellectual assent to the statement "God loves me." We know what His Word says! But our actual feelings can be very up and down... sometimes day to day...even moment by moment. We are hard-pressed to embrace that we are His children, His beloved, we are made in His image, etc.

Many of us are carrying messaging from long ago and perhaps recently about our abilities, appearance, talents, the value of our contributions. We're so attuned to the opinions of others—or to perceived opinions of others—and to defining ourselves and others by external things. And the constant detrimental working of the world around us can begin to erode what we believe about God's love and our worth. It's a non-trivial challenge to rest in God and abide in His LOVE FIRST...and let everything else flow from there.

The phrase **"unfailing love"** is used 39 times in the Bible—just two are about our own human desire for unfailing love. ALL of the remaining 37 are speaking of God alone. NOT ONE refers to humans being unfailingly loving. God—Father-Son-Holy Spirit— is the **only One** capable of loving you and me with love that never fails. Love that always endures. Love that is unceasing. Here's just a sampling—

God's unfailing love...leads, redeems, and delivers us;
provides refuge and strength; watches over, rescues, and saves
us; causes us to rejoice;
God's unfailing love enables us to not be shaken; is a source
of hope for us; is great, priceless, and trustworthy;
God's unfailing love derives from God's mercy and
compassion; satisfies, comforts, preserves, and comes to us;
supports us when we are "slipping," causes us to be thankful;
God's unfailing love is intertwined with God's complete
faithfulness, and **God's unfailing love** produces fruit.[4]

In Isaiah 43 (verses 1-7), the prophet is talking about The Lord Our
Only Savior, and says that the Lord Himself created you...formed
you...redeemed you...summoned you by name. You are HIS. In
verse 4, Isaiah quotes the Lord saying: **"You are precious and
honored in my sight...I love you...."**

You ARE precious...honored...loved...by the God who knit you
together in your mother's womb (Psalm 139:13). The Isaiah 43
passage continues by saying that we are "called by God's name"
and "created by Him for His glory." That speaks to purpose—but
LOVED by God comes FIRST.

As you meditate on the selected verse(s) for this week, may you
know and embrace God's GREAT and UNFAILING LOVE for
you.

---

[4] See Exodus 15:13; Psalm 6:4; 13:5; 18:50; 21:7; 26:3; 31:16; 32:10; 33:5;
33:18; 33:22; 36:7; 44:26; 48:9; 51:1; 52:8; 62:12; 77:8; 85:7; 90:14; 94:18;
107:8; 107:15; 107:21; 107:31; 109:26; 119:41; 119:76; 119:88; 130:7; 138:2;
143:8; 143:12; 147:11; Proverbs 19:22; 20:6; Isaiah 54:10; Lamentations 3:32;
Hosea 10:12.

Day 1
You are loved by the Father.

<u>John 16:27</u> The Father himself loves you because you have loved
me [Jesus] and have believed that I came from God.

Day 2
You are not condemned...Your sins are forgiven.
You are alive with Christ.

<u>Romans 8:34</u> Who then is the one who condemns? No one. Christ Jesus who died—more than that, who was raised to life—is at the right hand of God and is also interceding for us.

<u>Colossians 2:13-15</u> When you were dead in your sins...God made you alive with Christ. He forgave us all our sins, having canceled the charge of our legal indebtedness, which stood against us and condemned us; he has taken it away, nailing it to the cross.

Day 3
You are God's beneficiary—a co-heir with Christ.

Romans 8:16-17 The Spirit himself testifies with our spirit that we
are God's children. Now if we are children, then we are heirs—
heirs of God and co-heirs with Christ, if indeed we share in his
sufferings in order that we may also share in his glory.

Day 4
You are greatly loved by God, saved by His grace.

<u>Ephesians 2:4-5</u> But because of his great love for us, God, who is rich in mercy, made us alive with Christ even when we were dead in transgressions—it is by grace you have been saved.

Day 5
You can know God's will—His purpose—for you by giving yourself to Him to transform.

Romans 12:1-2 Therefore, I urge you, brothers and sisters, in view of God's mercy, to offer your bodies as a living sacrifice, holy and pleasing to God—this is your true and proper worship. Do not conform to the pattern of this world, but be transformed by the renewing of your mind. Then you will be able to test and approve what God's will is—his good, pleasing and perfect will.

Day 6
You can find refuge in God's love.

<u>Psalm 36:7</u> How priceless is your unfailing love, O God! People
take refuge in the shadow of your wings.

Day 7
Week 2 Prayer:

Lord, remind me today that Your LOVE for me is before and beyond my calling, purpose, accomplishments, failings, actions, and service. The fact that You loved and forgave me without my earning that love is truly remarkable. Help me to live in Your LOVE.

Erase any negativity that I'm holding onto—from my past, from the comments of others, from my own sense of unworthiness. May my self-definition come from my identity in Christ—not from external things.

Thank You that You are the only One who loves unfailingly. I am awed by the fact that Your love for me watches over and protects me. Your love saves and sustains me. Your love redeems me and gives me the strength I need. Your love comforts me. In all this, I worship You.

I take a moment to rest in the amazing truth that You call me by name. You forgive my sins. You do not condemn me, but You give me new life in Jesus. I am deeply grateful for Your grace and mercy toward me. I choose this day to find refuge in Your LOVE.

I pray all of this in trust in Your loving character,
Amen.

Optional Week 2 Activity:

Prayerfully meditate upon the fact that Scripture tells us that God's unfailing love...

> ...leads, redeems, and delivers us; provides refuge and strength; watches over, rescues, and saves us; causes us to rejoice; enables us to not be shaken; is a source of hope for us; is great, priceless, and trustworthy; derives from God's mercy and compassion; satisfies, comforts, preserves, and comes to us; supports us when we are "slipping," causes us to be thankful; is intertwined with God's complete faithfulness, and produces fruit.[5]

[Or, better yet, do your own word study of "unfailing love" in Scripture.]

---

[5] See Exodus 15:13; Psalm 6:4; 13:5; 18:50; 21:7; 26:3; 31:16; 32:10; 33:5; 33:18; 33:22; 36:7; 44:26; 48:9; 51:1; 52:8; 62:12; 77:8; 85:7; 90:14; 94:18; 107:8; 107:15; 107:21; 107:31; 109:26; 119:41; 119:76; 119:88; 130:7; 138:2; 143:8; 143:12; 147:11; Proverbs 19:22; 20:6; Isaiah 54:10; Lamentations 3:32; Hosea 10:12

Week Three—Loved by a Trustworthy God

How often do you find yourself thinking or feeling unappreciated, unfulfilled, trapped, less-than, driven to perform, less-than-gifted, feeling like you're not making enough of a difference? If you think/feel even a few of these things at least some of the time, you are not alone. And these comments derive from this pernicious habit we all seem to have of comparing ourselves with others. However, in comparing, we actually become less confident and more insecure.

In Scripture, there's a direct link between comparing and things like dissatisfaction, competition, poor relationships, envy, and lack of peace. There's also a direct link between keeping our focus on Christ and a healthy view of ourselves and others.

Lately, thanks to some inner work of the Holy Spirit, I have had the experience—wholly unrelated to my ability to "perform"—that GOD loves me; God LOVES me; God loves ME! Even in this very challenging season of the past few years that have spanned family illnesses, the deaths of my mother and my sister-in-law, less-than-successful surgeries for myself and my husband, and the subsequent temporary scaling back of work commitments that I thought gave me "value"—essentially being forced into less doing than being…it has become uncannily clear that God's love is above and beyond and prior to what I DO. God's love is also separate from whether or not He answers all of my requests and desperate pleas with a "yes." There have been a lot of "no's" in my life in recent years from God. In spite of this, I am more and more convinced that His deep love surpasses all…is unfailing…and is trustworthy in and in spite of circumstances and my own abilities.

25

You may be in a similar challenging season. **I'm here to tell you that God's love is trustworthy.**

Once we know…experience…believe…rest in…are healed by… understand…are restored and transformed by God's love…**it WILL spill over into action.** Actions like loving God back and loving ourselves and loving our neighbors:

In Matthew 22:37-40, Jesus Himself says that the actions that matter most are: **"Love the Lord your God with all your heart and with all your soul and with all your mind"** *and* **"Love your neighbor as yourself."**

Jesus' disciple John says it this way in 1 John 4:7-12: *"Dear friends,* **let us love one another, for love comes from God.** *Everyone who loves has been born of God and knows God…This is love: not that we loved God, but that he loved us and sent his Son as an atoning sacrifice for our sins. Dear friends,* **since God so loved us, we also ought to love one another.** *No one has ever seen God; but if we love one another, God lives in us and his love is made complete in us."*

As you reflect on this week's verses, in cooperation with His Spirit, hold fast to the fact that **"God's love has been poured out into our hearts through the Holy Spirit, who has been given to us"** (Romans 5:5).

Day 1
You are named by God...called...loved.

Isaiah 45:3 I will give you hidden treasures, riches stored in secret places, so that you may know that I am the Lord, the God of Israel, who summons you by name.

Jude 1:1 ...To those who have been called, who are loved in God the Father and kept for Jesus Christ...

Day 2
You have received freely from God...so you can be generous to others.

<u>Matthew 10:8</u> Freely you have received; freely give.

Day 3
You are God's child, led by His Spirit.

Romans 8:14 For those who are led by the Spirit of God are the children of God.

Day 4
God's love for you is boundless!

<u>Psalm 36:5</u> Your love, Lord, reaches to the heavens, Your faithfulness to the skies.

Day 5
You have been chosen by God…to bear lasting fruit.

<u>John 15:16</u> You did not choose me, but I chose you and appointed you so that you might go and bear fruit—fruit that will last—and so that whatever you ask in my name the Father will give you.

Day 6
Take a moment now to read these verses aloud.
Insert your name in each blank space. Say it over at least twice.
Savor the thought contained in these words direct from God to
your heart:

May our Lord Jesus Christ himself and God our Father, who loved
YOU (Name)_____ and by His grace gave YOU
eternal encouragement and good hope, encourage YOUR heart and
strengthen YOU in every good deed and word.
2 Thessalonians 2:16-17

Day 7
Week 3 Prayer:

Trustworthy Lord,
Remove any thoughts and feelings of unworthiness. May You
alone be my Source of holy affirmation and daily encouragement,
May I rest in the wondrous truth that I am your handiwork, called
and purposed by You to be in the places and with the people You
have chosen for me to work/love/interact.

Remove any tendency to compare myself with others. Replace it
with a constant and strong sense of Your Presence and Your delight
in me. I know that I am secure in You.

Remind me of the fact that You love me. Help me to love You
honestly and completely so that I might love myself well and love
others as You intend. Live in me. Make Your love complete in me.
I choose today to abide in You. To trust You as the Source of my
life and strength. Make me able, by Your Spirit, to experience
Your complete joy.

May the fruit I bear come from my connection to You so that it
makes a meaningful difference—reflecting Your character. I choose
today to give freely because I am one to whom You have already
freely given. I choose to be led by Your Spirit, as Your child. I
choose today to soak in the fact that "Your love, Lord, reaches to
the heavens, Your faithfulness to the skies" (Psalm 36:5).

I am so very grateful that You have chosen...appointed...purposed
me to do Your work in this world. Make me able.
Amen.

Optional Week 3 Activity:
Reflect:

What is one way you are loving God these days?
What is one way you are loving yourself these days?
How does this spill over into loving your neighbor?

Week Four—Freedom in Christ

I just ran across these convicting words from *The Joy of Serving God*: "Live a life of comparison and competition and you end up with no joy at all."[6] Again, I'm faced with the realization that my tendency to compare with someone else—using others as my standard—either for thinking I'm better than they are (pride) or thinking I'm not as good as they are (still self-focused!), is related to envy and breeds dissatisfaction in my soul. Comparison and envy and competition are strongholds—ones that keep us in a bondage that God never intended for us. Keeping our focus on how we measure up to others leads to destruction—us and them. The study guide's authors go on to say (in the chapter called "Comparison: the Killjoy of Servanthood"), "Envy is disliking God's goodness to someone else and dismissing God's goodness to me. Envy is desire plus resentment. It not only seeks self-gratification, but it seeks to diminish the one I envy...It can extend to everything—even another person's spirituality, giftedness, or servanthood."[7]

The remedy? Ask God to change your heart and mind (James 4:2). Ask Him to change your focus—to help us "fix our eyes on Jesus, the author and perfecter of our faith" (Hebrews 12:1-3). God is the only stronghold Who works to save and shelter us (Psalm 9:9; 18:2; 27:1). Paul says we have, in Christ, "divine power to demolish [all other] strongholds"...and "we take captive every

---

[6] *Gifts: The Joy of Serving God* by John Ortberg, Laurie Pederson, Judson Poling; part of the Willow Creek *Pursuing Spiritual Transformation* series. Page 68.
[7] Ibid. Page 66.

thought and make it obedient to Christ"...and we stop "judging by appearances" (2 Corinthians 10:1-7).

Theologian Dallas Willard said:

> *"The most important thing in your life is not what you do; it's who you become. That's what you will take into eternity. You are an unceasing spiritual being with an eternal destiny in God's great universe..."*[8]

> *"The 'with God' life is not a life of more religious activities or devotions or trying to be good. It is a life of inner peace and contentment for your soul with the maker and manager of the universe."*[9]

> *"That's the whole point of tending to the soul—to fill us so completely with his presence that the brilliance of his love shines through us...God wants you to focus on him. To be with him. 'Abide in me.' Just relax and learn to enjoy his presence."*[10]

We do this moment-by-moment, day-by-day...not all at once. God says your significance is rooted in who you are—not in what you do. Jesus promises that as we stay connected to Him and as we obey Him, His joy will be in us and that joy will be complete. And, obedience looks like obeying His command: "Love each other as I have loved you." When you aren't clear on the next thing, you can still be committed to loving those around you.

Bask this week in your freedom in Christ and its implications for your life.

---

[8] As quoted in *Soul Keeping*, John Ortberg, eBook Location: 1,779.
[9] Ibid. Location: 1,795.
[10] Ibid. Location: 1,797.

Day 1
You are not condemned but free.

<u>Romans 8:1-2</u> Therefore, there is now no condemnation for those who are in Christ Jesus, because through Christ Jesus the law of the Spirit who gives life has set you free from the law of sin and death.

Day 2
You are redeemed…forgiven...completely…by grace.

<u>Ephesians 1:7-8</u> In him we have redemption through his blood, the forgiveness of sins, in accordance with the riches of God's grace that he lavished on us.

Day 3
You are His child. You are an heir…and Jesus' sibling.

Galatians 4:7 So you are no longer a slave, but God's child; and since you are his child, God has made you also an heir.

Hebrews 2:11 Both the one who makes people holy and those who are made holy are of the same family. So Jesus is not ashamed to call them brothers and sisters.

Day 4
You are set free by God Himself in Jesus.

<u>Acts 13:39</u> Through him everyone who believes is set free from every sin, a justification you were not able to obtain under the law of Moses.

Day 5
You are free from condemnation.

<u>John 3:17-18a</u> For God did not send his Son into the world to condemn the world, but to save the world through him. Whoever believes in him is not condemned.

Day 6
Take a moment now to read these verses aloud.
Insert your name in each blank space. Say it over at least twice.
Savor the thought contained in these words direct from
God to your heart:

So, You (Name)_____ are no longer a slave, but God's
child; and since You (Name) _____are his
child, God has made YOU (Name) _____ also an
heir—an inheritor of His Kingdom.
Galatians 4:7

Day 7
Week 4 Prayer:

Lord, take away any tendencies I have toward jealousy and envy
of others—for who they are or what they have. Rewire my mind
so that I am increasingly able to "fix my eyes on Jesus." You have
authored my faith—please perfect it.

Destroy any strongholds that are keeping me from You and
Your redemptive work in my heart. Make Yourself my only
stronghold—saving and sheltering me. Enable me by Your divine
power to choose today to "take captive every thought and make it
obedient to Christ" (2 Corinthians 10:1-7).

May my character reflect You. May my actions mirror You. May
my thoughts be Your thoughts.

Show me where I am busy with activity—with doing—but not
paying attention to being. I want to be a vessel filled with You. A
person whose soul allows Your light to shine through.

I choose today to find my primary identity in Jesus. I commit to
stop trying to "earn" Your love. I simply will live the with-Jesus
life, knowing that You have, do, and will always love me.
I pause now to sit in the truth of my freedom from condemnation
and my complete forgiveness from You. [PAUSE to reflect.]
Amen.

Optional Week 4 Activity:

Take a moment to reflect—What intentional practices do you pursue so that you remain connected to Jesus?

God's gracious love. It blows the mind. From previous weeks, you know you are "precious and honored in God's sight." God loves you "completely." Remember and meditate today on the fact that Jesus loves you "always" as you also pray that the Lord would help you "always" remain in His love by abiding with Him. Today, receive the Lord's love…abide in Jesus and "walk in the way of love." (Ephesians 5:2)

Week Five—Abide: Set Your Eyes on Jesus

We are promised that if we earnestly seek God, we will find Him (1 Chronicles 28:9; Deuteronomy 4:29). We have the power of the Holy Spirit to help us with this. Romans 8:5-6 tells us that "Those who live according to the flesh have their minds set on what the flesh desires; but those who live in accordance with the Spirit have their minds set on what the Spirit desires. The mind governed by the flesh is death, but the mind governed by the Spirit is life and peace." A related verse says much the same thing, reminding us again that what we think about—what we set our minds on— determines our level of peace: "You [God] will keep in perfect peace those whose minds are steadfast, because they trust in You" (Isaiah 26:3).

When our eyes are on ourselves or on others or on comparing ourselves with others, we lose heart. We feed our imagined fears; we keep track of all the wrong things; we judge and are judged in return; we reap what we sow in our relationships; we exchange joy and peace for deception and discontent and pretense. (2 Samuel 22:46; 1 Corinthians 13:5; Matthew 7:1-2; Luke 6:37; Proverbs 12:20).

However, when our eyes are on God...eagerly seeking Him, we experience transformation, power by the Spirit, life, peace, and are centered in His love. Our perspective changes from our and others' human frailties and limitations to resting in the sovereignty of the Creator of the universe. We can ask God to keep us loyal and devoted to Him AND lean into the power of His Spirit to govern our minds and hearts. Day by day. Week by week. Month by month. Year by year.

Jesus' instructions in John 15 are useful here. He says:

> *"Remain in me, as I also remain in you. No branch can bear fruit by itself; it must remain in the vine. Neither can you bear fruit unless you remain in me.*
>
> *"I—Jesus—am the vine; you are the branches. If you remain in me and I in you, you will bear much fruit; apart from me you can do nothing…This is to my Father's glory, that you bear much fruit, showing yourselves to be my disciples.*
>
> *"As the Father has loved me, so have I loved you. Now remain in my love. If you keep my commands, you will remain in my love, just as I have kept my Father's commands and remain in his love. I have told you this so that my joy may be in you and that your joy may be complete. My command is this: Love each other as I have loved you. Greater love has no one than this: to lay down one's life for one's friends…You did not choose me, but I chose you and appointed you so that you might go and bear fruit—fruit that will last—and so that whatever you ask in my name the Father will give you. This is my command: Love each other" (verses 4-17).*

In these last teachings to His disciples before His death, what does Jesus say are the most important things He wants them, and us, to remember?

- You are loved
- Abide in Jesus
- Love one another
- Bear much fruit
- Experience complete joy
- Know that you are chosen/appointed…to bear lasting fruit
- Love each other

Our objective is not fruit-bearing. Our aim is to abide…to stay

connected …firmly attached. From THAT comes the fruit.

Apart from Me. We cannot bear fruit—character fruit—like compassion, kindness, humility, gentleness, patience (Colossians 3:12)—on our own. With Jesus, we will be abundantly fruitful—which glorifies God. When you cut off a branch or put cut flowers in a vase, how long before these things wither? How long before they die? Once severed, a stem cannot provide life to itself. Jesus says it is the same with us. If we are out of contact with… disconnected from…Him, we wither and we die—spiritually.

This week, remember that your connection to Jesus is not just part of it—it is **THE thing** that matters, THE thing that empowers. Abiding is the key to having our minds "governed by" His Spirit and living into His "life and peace."

Day 1
You will find God when you love and seek Him.

<u>Proverbs 8:17</u> I love those who love me, and those who seek me find me.

Day 2
You are complete in Christ.

<u>Colossians 2:10</u> ...and in Christ you have been brought to fullness. He is the head over every power and authority.

Day 3
You are dearly loved…and chosen…by God.

<u>Colossians 3:12</u> Therefore, as God's chosen people, holy and dearly loved, clothe yourselves with compassion, kindness, humility, gentleness and patience.

Day 4
You are loved by God...You are chosen by Him.

1 Thessalonians 1:4-5 For we know, brothers and sisters loved by God, that he has chosen you, because our gospel came to you not simply with words but also with power, with the Holy Spirit and deep conviction.

Day 5
Jesus provides the strength we need.

<u>Philippians 4:13</u> I can do all this through him who gives me strength.

Day 6

Take a moment now to read the following verse aloud.
Insert your name in each blank space. Say it over at least twice.
Savor the thought contained in these words direct from
God to your heart:

But You (Name)_____ are a chosen person, an
integral part of a chosen people, a royal priesthood, a holy nation...
YOU (Name)_____ are God's special possession—chosen
to declare the praises of Him who called YOU—rescued YOU
(Name)_____ out of darkness into His wonderful light.
1 Peter 2:9

Day 7
Week 5 Prayer:

Sovereign Lord,
In this quiet moment, I earnestly seek You, knowing I will find
You. Through Your Spirit, give me Your life and Your peace. Keep
my mind focused on You. Remove my fears. Replace them with
calm and tranquility.

I choose today to rest in Your sovereignty. I remind myself that
You make me complete. You fill me. You continue to love me,
dearly. I remain chosen by You. I can live in faith and power by
Your Holy Spirit. I am Your child. I am Your special possession.

I praise You that You have rescued me out of darkness into Your
brilliant light. May I, in Your strength, continue to set my eyes on
You this week.

In Your peace-filled Name,
Amen.

Optional Week 5 Activity:

How might you live with a "mind governed by the Spirit,"
experiencing supernatural "life and peace" as you seek and set
your eyes on Jesus this week?

Week Six—The New Fruit-Bearing Self

There is a sense as you approach this week and the next that finishing these twelve weeks will require commitment and work on your part. You're not far wrong!

When you consider habit-formation, the goal is to create (or replace) behaviors that become or have become automatic. It takes intentional commitment and a set of practices, repeated over time, to create new pathways in our brains before we have a new routine. According to *The Power of Habit*: "Put another way, a habit is a formula our brain automatically follows: When I see CUE, I will do ROUTINE in order to get a REWARD. To re-engineer that formula, we need to begin making choices again. And the easiest way to do this, according to study after study, is to have a plan. Within psychology, these plans are known as 'implementation intentions.'"[11]

The God who created us—formed us with great intention—knows human nature. He knows how good habits (and bad ones) become hardwired in us. Again, we find in Scripture much that can guide us in this as we become purposeful about how we live.

We are told by Paul in Ephesians to "put off your old self, which is being corrupted by its deceitful desires, to be made new in the attitude of your minds; and to put on the new self, created to be like God in true righteousness and holiness." In Romans, he says, "Make every effort to do what leads to peace and to mutual

---

[11] *The Power of Habit: Why We Do What We Do in Life and Business* by Charles Duhigg, eBook Location 4524.

edification." Peter and the writer of Hebrews echo the same thing: "Make every effort to live in peace with everyone and to be holy." Paul again: "Strive for full restoration, encourage one another, be of one mind, live in peace. And the God of love and peace will be with you" (Ephesians 4:20-24; Romans 14:19; 2 Peter 3:14; Hebrews 12:14; 2 Corinthians 13:11).

In each case, this "put off, strive for, make every effort" are commands which involve work and active commitment. There are no exceptions (note it says "everyone"). We are called to be disciplined, as ones going into training. It's about putting off old habits of self-focus and unbelief and REPLACING them with new ones, empowered by God—in the power of the Holy Spirit, it's not just sheer straining on our part: "But the fruit of the Spirit [produced by HIM] is love, joy, peace, patience, kindness, goodness, faithfulness, gentleness, and self-control. Against such things there is no law. Those who belong to Christ Jesus have crucified the flesh with its passions and desires. Since we live by the Spirit, let us keep in step with the Spirit" (Galatians 5:22-25).

A thought that has been hugely helpful for me in recent months, thanks to JhéDienne Adams, a University Ministry intern at our church who lived with us a few years ago. She learned this from Jill Edward at a retreat [adapted]:

> *"We have two identities in Christ. We are beloved children of God, and we are servants of God. They are both true, but the order in which we believe them matters. If I know myself to be a servant of God first, I will serve to earn my daughtership. If I know myself first as his daughter, I am moved to serve him. We are to know ourselves first as beloved daughter of God, and only then are we truly free to serve him, and to serve him faithfully."*

I can honestly say that I often have this reversed...thinking of myself (consciously or subconsciously) as a servant of God first... which leaves me trying to achieve things to earn God's favor and human recognition...when instead, I need to (as JhéDienne reminded me not long ago) "rest at His feet from the privileged position of being His beloved daughter." I also think that this is a particular challenge for some church communities.

I hope that you want to live the WITH-JESUS-LIFE. The life of abiding. Remaining. Resting in and obeying Him. Letting Him help you BE and become who you really are. The security of that connection to Christ enables you to then freely live out your unique purpose....and to live as He lived.

There is a Jeremiah 31:3 card that sits on my bathroom counter. It says: **I will always love you. -God.** Dolly Parton and Whitney Houston have nothing on the God of the universe who said it first...and always...for eternity...to you and to me.

Stay the course. Make every effort to connect with the Lord through the following Scriptures and practices.

Day 1
You are much loved by God.

<u>1 John 4:11</u> Dear friends, since God so loved us, we also ought to love one another.

Day 2
You are free and accepted, so go live differently.

Psalm 116:16 Truly I am your servant, Lord…you have freed
me from my chains.

John 8:10-11 Jesus straightened up and asked her, "Woman, where
are they? Has no one condemned you?" "No one, sir," she said.
"Then neither do I condemn you," Jesus declared. "Go now and
leave your life of sin."

Day 3
Rejoice...in the Lord, you can live a life of encouragement,
love, unity, and peace.

<u>2 Corinthians 13:11</u> Finally, brothers and sisters, rejoice! Strive
for full restoration, encourage one another, be of one mind, live in
peace. And the God of love and peace will be with you.

Day 4
You can choose to put off your old self and be made new.

Ephesians 4:22-24 You were taught, with regard to your former way of life, to put off your old self, which is being corrupted by its deceitful desires; to be made new in the attitude of your minds; and to put on the new self, created to be like God in true righteousness and holiness.

Day 5
The more You keep in step with God's Spirit, the more you will be able to bear the fruit of love, joy, peace, etc.

Galatians 5:22-25 But the fruit of the Spirit is love, joy, peace, patience, kindness, goodness, faithfulness, gentleness and self-control. Against such things there is no law. Those who belong to Christ Jesus have crucified the flesh with its passions and desires. Since we live by the Spirit, let us keep in step with the Spirit.

Day 6
Take a moment now to read these verses aloud.
Insert your name in each blank space. Say it over at least twice.
Savor the thought contained in these words direct from
God to your heart:

For God created YOUR inmost being (Name)_____; He
knit YOU together in YOUR mother's womb. I praise you, [Lord]
because I am fearfully and wonderfully made; your works are
wonderful, I know that full well. My frame was not hidden from
you when I was made in the secret place, when I was woven
together in the depths of the earth.
Psalm 139:13-16

Day 7
Week 6 Prayer:

God Who loves me,
Help me to remain dedicated to the study of Your Word and Your
truth. Form in me patterns that align with Your goodness and Your
intent for my life. Empower me to be purposeful in that
habit-formation, denying myself the things that are distractions
and temptations and being intentional about pursuit of the
newness You intend.

Make me new—in the attitude of my mind—so that I can be
righteous and holy. I commit today to pursue peace and to
encourage others. I choose to keep short accounts, to pursue love
and justice, to be a person of forgiveness and restoration. I know I
need Your help in all of this!

I desire to be increasingly full of Your love, joy, peace, patience,
kindness, goodness, faithfulness, gentleness, and self-control. Help
me to keep in step with Your Spirit each and every day. I will be
Your person of unity, a peacemaker who brings a non-anxious
presence wherever I find myself. I know I cannot do any of this
without the strength and courage You provide.

Thank You, Prince of Peace,
Amen.

Optional Week 6 Activity:

What is one step you might take this week to "make every effort to do what leads to peace and mutual edification," striving for "full restoration"?

Week Seven—God's Faithfulness & Everlasting Covenant of Love

According to psychologist Jonah Paquette (author of *Awestruck*) experiencing awe (both the sense of vastness and of transcendence) is complex and essential to our well-being. In addition, awe decreases our ego and stress, increases our ability to be generous and kind, and improves our relationships, contentment, and happiness.[12]

Some practices that Paquette recommends for experiencing the benefits of awe: stay/remain with the feeling of wonder as long as you can without moving on to the next thing; slow down; check in with all of your senses; disconnect with technology; take walks; journal about what has been awe-inspiring.[13]

Not surprisingly, these findings align with what the Lord has been saying to us and showing to us—through His Creation, His Word, in Jesus—for millennia. "Many, Lord my God, are the wonders you have done, the things you planned for us. None can compare with You; were I to speak and tell of your deeds, they would be too many to declare" (Psalm 40:5). Many. Wonders. No comparison. Too many. Awe. Wonder. Amazement. Perspective.

I hope you have a sense now by week seven of saturating yourself in God's Words to you that the Lord is working wonders in your

---

[12] *Six Ways to Incorporate Awe into Your Daily Life*, by Teja Pattabhiraman, March 2, 2021. Greater Good Science Center.
[13] Ibid.

life through a refocus of your mind and heart. I hope that you are clearer on who God is, how much He truly loves you, and more grounded in that unfailing love. Your continuation of this devotional and its Scriptures and practices is helping you linger, to engage with a deep experience of awe as you contemplate yourself in relation to the gracious, compassionate Lord. Perhaps you are also seeing improvements in your relationships and decreases in your stress—all of which are the results of "many, Lord, my God, are the wonders you have done, the things you planned for us...."

The translated phrase "everlasting love" is only used once in the New International Version of the Bible. That once is about God alone: "The Lord appeared to us in the past saying: 'I have loved you with an everlasting love; I have drawn you with unfailing kindness.'" When you look at the words faithful and faithfulness, over 120 of the 202 mentions are about God alone. Of the remaining 80, 25 are about God asking us to be faithful to Him or about the inability of humankind to be faithful. Over and over, we hear of the "kindness and faithfulness" of God, that He is "abounding in love and faithfulness." (Genesis 24:27; 32:10; Exodus 34:6; 2 Samuel 2:6; 2 Samuel 15:20)

Faithfulness—a less-used word in our current cultural vocabulary—echoes steadfast and long-lasting trustworthiness and loyalty in relationships, commitments, promises. Aren't you glad that God embodies that word more than any human could ever hope to? When He makes a promise, a covenant, a commitment, He keeps it!

Meditate this week on the verses provided, keeping in mind the words of Deuteronomy 7:9: "Know therefore that the Lord your God is God; **He is the faithful God, keeping His covenant of love** to a thousand generations of those who love Him and keep His commandments."

Day 1
**You are seen and embraced by a compassionate, loving,
faithful, gracious, forgiving Lord.**

Exodus 34:6-7 …"The Lord, the Lord, the compassionate and
gracious God, slow to anger, abounding in love and faithfulness,
maintaining love to thousands, and forgiving wickedness,
rebellion and sin…"

Day 2
You do not belong to this world...you have been chosen by Jesus.

John 15:19 If you belonged to the world, it would love you as its own. As it is, you do not belong to the world, but I have chosen you out of the world.

Day 3
**You are not condemned....the Lord has rescued you...He is
your refuge.**

Psalm 34:22 The Lord will rescue his servants; no one who takes
refuge in him will be condemned.

Day 4
You have been called, chosen by God.

<u>Isaiah 41:9</u> I took you from the ends of the earth, from its farthest corners I called you. I said, 'You are my servant'; I have chosen you and have not rejected you.

Day 5
May you know God's loving, kind faithfulness today.

<u>2 Samuel 2:6</u> May the Lord now show you kindness and faithfulness…

Day 6

Take a moment now to read the following verses aloud. Yes, aloud.
Insert your name in each blank space. Say it over at least twice.
Savor the thought contained in these words direct from
God to your heart:

(Name) _____ See what great love the Father
has lavished on YOU, that YOU are called a CHILD of GOD! And
that is what YOU are! (Name)_____, now YOU are
a CHILD of GOD, and what YOU will be has not yet been made
known. But YOU can know that when Christ appears, YOU WILL
be LIKE HIM, for YOU shall see Him as He is.

1 John 3:1-2

Day 7
Week 7 Prayer:

Lord of lords and King of kings.
I take a moment now to sit in awe of You. I name aloud things I
worship about Your greatness, Your transcendence, Your holiness,
Your wonders, Your sacrificial love for me.
[PAUSE in awe and worship.]

Thank You that just stopping to do this brings me much-needed
perspective—on You and on my life. Thank You that these past
weeks of saturating myself in Your Word is changing me from the
inside out. Thank You for new clarity about You, Your love for me,
Your compassion, Your ability to relieve my stress, Your purpose
for my life.

I am truly grateful for Your everlasting love. Unending. Eternal.
Undiminishing. Faithful. Boundless. Thank You for Your lasting
covenant promises to me. I recommit to believing that You see me,
You love me, You forgive me.

I acknowledge that I am not of this world but that You have
rescued me and set me apart for Yourself. I also embrace that Your
call upon my life is to return to the world as Your reconciling
ambassador of love and grace. May I be a worthy representative of
Your love to others that they might be drawn to You.
Amen.

Optional Week 7 Activity:

Pick an awe practice and do it today: sit with the feeling of wonder; slow down; check in with all of your senses; disconnect with technology; take a walk; journal about what has been awe-inspiring. See how this experience helps you get new and needed perspective on the Lord and on your life.

Week Eight—God is Steadfast: Love & Faithfulness Go Together

There are times when we do not feel God's love or believe that He is with us. The Psalmist talks of such an experience when he says, "Lord, where is Your former great love, which in Your faithfulness you swore to David?" (Psalm 89:49). God is not upset by those kinds of questions from us. But He answers continuously through His Word, the Bible, with promise after promise, assurance after assurance, steadfastness and consistency: "The Lord is righteous in all His ways and faithful in all He does." "He remains faithful forever." "A bruised reed He will not break, and a smoldering wick He will not snuff out." "For the Lord is good and His love endures forever; His faithfulness continues through all generations." (Psalm 145:17; Psalm 146:6; Isaiah 42:3; Psalm 100:5)

As Beth Moore says so well in her *Breaking Free* study guide: "God's love is unfailing, so any time we perceive He does not love us, our perceptions are wrong. Anything we perceive about God that does not match up with (1) the truth of Scripture and (2) the portrayal of His character in Scripture—is a lie."[14]

We do have an enemy of our souls whom Jesus calls a murderer, a liar, and the father of lies (John 8:44). This enemy is evil and tempts both us and Jesus to believe that the Lord is not who He says He is and that His promises are not valid (Matthew 4, 13, Luke 4, Ephesians 4). However, we are given powerful spiritual armor to stand up to this enemy: strength in God and His power, truth (belt), righteousness (breastplate), the gospel of peace

---

[14] *Breaking Free* updated edition, Week 8, by Beth Moore.

Week Eight—God is Steadfast: Love & Faithfulness Go Together

(shoes), faith (shield), salvation (helmet), the Word of God (sword of the Spirit), prayer in the Spirit on all occasions, alertness (Ephesians 5:10-20).

As the Psalmist says: "Love and faithfulness meet together; righteousness and peace kiss each other" (Psalm 85:10). Scriptures often speak of God's love for us and His faithfulness toward us in the same sentence or phrase. God's love, compassion, graciousness, kindness, faithfulness are intricately connected, and Scripture says that His love and faithfulness are protection and salvation for us (Psalm 57, 61). Many times, when we read of these characteristics of the Lord, we also are told that He is "slow to anger," that He "remembers" us, and that these traits endure "forever" (Psalm 86, 98, 117).

God's Word is clear that we haven't earned nor deserved all of this wonderful grace and love and affection from God. "But God demonstrates his own love for us in this: While we were still sinners, Christ died for us" (Romans 5:8). "For God so loved the world that he gave his one and only Son, that whoever believes in him shall not perish but have eternal life. For God did not send his Son into the world to condemn the world, but to save the world through him" (John 3:16-17). The ultimate sacrifice. Out of love. Undeserved. Unearned.

So, there is nothing you can do to make God love you more than He does. There is nothing you can do to make God love you less than He does. He loves you. Period. Use the following verses to continue to remind yourself of what is TRUE about God, and about yourself in relation to God...to counteract any lies about the Lord's character...while basking in the knowledge that nothing you have done or can do can change God's love for you.

Day 1
You are the Lord's treasured possession.

Deuteronomy 7:6 For you are a people holy to the Lord your God.
The Lord your God has chosen you out of all the peoples on the
face of the earth to be his people, his treasured possession.

Day 2
You can trust that the Lord is faithful and forever trustworthy.

Psalm 145:17 The Lord is righteous in all his ways and faithful in
all he does.

Psalm 146:6 He is the Maker of heaven and earth, the sea, and
everything in them—he remains faithful forever.

Day 3
You are loved, pardoned, and forgiven by a wondrous, compassionate Lord who is full of grace and mercy.

<u>Psalm 111:4</u> He has caused his wonders to be remembered; the Lord is gracious and compassionate.

<u>Micah 7:18</u> Who is a God like you, who pardons sin and forgives the transgression of the remnant of his inheritance? You do not stay angry forever but delight to show mercy.

Day 4
The Lord will care kindly for you and for those suffering injustice.

Isaiah 42:3-4 A bruised reed he will not break, and a smoldering wick he will not snuff out. In faithfulness he will bring forth justice; he will not falter or be discouraged till he establishes justice on earth.

Day 5
You can rely on the faithfulness and love of God.

<u>Psalm 26:3</u> For I have always been mindful of your unfailing love
and have lived in reliance on your faithfulness.

God saves you in His faithful love.

<u>Psalm 57:3</u> He sends from heaven and saves me, rebuking those
who hotly pursue me—God sends forth his love
and his faithfulness.

Day 6

Take a moment now to read the following verses aloud.
Insert your name in each blank space. Say it over at least twice.
Savor the thought contained in these words direct from
God to your heart:

YOU (Name)_____ are the one the Lord loves—
YOU rest (You are carried) between His shoulders.
Deuteronomy 33:12b

God has said, (Name)_____ "Never will I leave
you; never will I forsake you." (Name)_____YOU
are never alone.
Hebrews 13:5

Day 7
Week 8 Prayer:

Faithful Lord,
I praise You that Your love and faithfulness are protection and salvation for me. I find it amazing that You "remember" me. For my sake, I am glad that You are "slow to anger." In moments when I forget Your love and faithfulness to me, I remind myself that you are unchanging, steadfast, consistent. I'm comforted by the fact that Your loving kindness and faithfulness are not dependent on me, my emotions, my circumstances, my belief. I rest in the fact that I cannot do anything to make You love me more or love me less. I again choose You, Your death and resurrection on my behalf, Your pardon, Your salvation, Your eternal life. May I be a beacon of exactly that redemption and hope to others with whom I have contact today.

I take a moment to sit in the deep well of Your grace depicted in these verses: "But God demonstrates his own love for us in this: While we were still sinners, Christ died for us" (Romans 5:8). "For God so loved the world that he gave his one and only Son, that whoever believes in him shall not perish but have eternal life. For God did not send his Son into the world to condemn the world, but to save the world through him" (John 3:16-17). [PAUSE to embrace these truths.] Clothe me in Your holy armor. Nudge me to pray on all occasions and in all circumstances.

Make me the kind of disciple who tells the truth—Your Truth, who is generous—a faithful steward of all You have given me, who is careful about the words that come out of my mouth, who encourages and builds up others for their health and betterment, who is kind, compassionate, and forgiving as I model Christlikeness.

I trust that You are trustworthy, that I am treasured by You, and that You have truly set me free. I ask that You bring forth justice…and help me know where You would have me be an agent of justice today.
Amen.

Optional Week 8 Activity:

Pick a current challenge you face. Pray for the armor of God to
help you stand up to that challenge in the power of His Spirit:
strength in God and His power, truth (belt), righteousness
(breastplate), the gospel of peace (shoes), faith (shield), salvation
(helmet), the Word of God (sword of the Spirit), prayer in the Spirit
on all occasions, alertness (Ephesians 5:10-20).

Week Nine—Freely Responding in Obedience

Our own faithlessness is not sufficient reason for God to abandon us. Hard to believe, since we have a tendency to withdraw our affection from those who have proven faithless to us. But as Nehemiah says of the ongoing stubbornness of Israel: "They refused to listen and failed to remember the miracles you performed among them. They became stiff-necked and in their rebellion appointed a leader in order to return to their slavery. **But you are a forgiving God, gracious and compassionate, slow to anger and abounding in love.** Therefore you did not desert them, even when they cast for themselves an image of a calf and said, 'This is your god, who brought you up out of Egypt,' or when they committed awful blasphemies. **Because of your great compassion you did not abandon them in the wilderness…You gave your good Spirit to instruct them**" (Nehemiah 9:17-20, emphasis mine).

In Luke 4:16-21, we read of Jesus on the Sabbath, in the synagogue in His home town, reading of His own purpose as prophesied in Isaiah:

> *"The Spirit of the Lord is on me,*
> *because he has anointed me*
> *to proclaim good news to the poor.*
> *He has sent me to proclaim **freedom** for the prisoners*
> *and recovery of sight for the blind,*
> *to set the oppressed **free**,*
> *to proclaim the year of the Lord's favor."*

Week Nine—Freely Responding in Obedience

Jesus knew the role for which He was anointed, and that role includes healing and freedom for us—for those imprisoned, for the oppressed. He voluntarily came in love to release us from anything that might hold us in bondage...to offer life in Himself.

This doesn't mean that we then have license to do as we please without concern for consequences. God desires that we unreservedly respond to His love by following His Word in the power of the Spirit so that we might have life abundantly (John 10:10). "It is for freedom that Christ has set us free. Stand firm, then, and do not let yourselves be burdened again by a yoke of slavery"..."You, my brothers and sisters, were called to be free. But do not use your freedom to indulge the flesh; rather, serve one another humbly in love" (Galatians 5:1, 13). There's a charge and challenge to use our freedom in Christ for the benefit of others through humble, loving service.

In his instructions for living as Christ-followers, Paul tells us in Ephesians 4: to be truth-telling people, generous, intentional about our speech—building others up for their benefit, marked by kindness, compassion, forgiveness—that models Christ's complete forgiveness to us.

Choose this week to live in the freedom and response that both issue from God's love.

Day 1
You are not only set free from sin, you are free in Christ to live differently.

Romans 6:18, 22 You have been set free from sin and have become slaves to righteousness...But now that you have been set free from sin and have become slaves of God, the benefit you reap leads to holiness, and the result is eternal life.

Galatians 5:1 [Freedom in Christ] It is for freedom that Christ has set us free. Stand firm, then, and do not let yourselves be burdened again by a yoke of slavery.

Day 2
You have been rescued.

<u>Colossians 1:13</u> For he has rescued us from the dominion of darkness and brought us into the kingdom of the Son he loves.

Day 3
**You may approach God, through Jesus, with freedom
and confidence.**

Ephesians 3:10-12 His intent was that now, through the church, the
manifold wisdom of God should be made known to the rulers and
authorities in the heavenly realms, according to his eternal purpose
that he accomplished in Christ Jesus our Lord. In him and through
faith in him we may approach God with freedom and confidence.

Day 4
You are forgiven and redeemed from the pit.

<u>1 John 1:9</u> If we confess our sins, he is faithful and just and will forgive us our sins and purify us from all unrighteousness.

<u>Psalm 103:2-4</u> Praise the Lord, my soul, and forget not all his benefits—who forgives all your sins and heals all your diseases, who redeems your life from the pit and crowns you with love and compassion.

Day 5
You are free.

<u>John 8:36</u> So if the Son sets you free, you will be free indeed.

Day 6
Take a moment now to read these verses aloud as if the Lord
is speaking directly to you through them today.
Savor the thought contained in these words direct from
God to your heart:

Deuteronomy 5:33 Walk in obedience to all that the Lord your God
has commanded you, so that you may live and prosper and prolong
your days in the land that you will possess.

Deuteronomy 8:6 Observe the commands of the Lord your God,
walking in obedience to him and revering him.

Day 7
Week 9 Prayer:

Affectionate Lord who does not abandon me,
Help me to listen and to hear You. Prevent me from becoming
stiff-necked toward You and Your commands. Remind me of Your
miracles—historical and in my own life and the lives of my loved
ones. Thank You that You do not desert me but continue to offer
me Your boundless love. Continue to give me "Your good Spirit"
to teach me.

In the great freedom I have in You, help me be ever faithful in
responding with obedience. I desire to have that life-abundant You
promise. Make me a loyal servant of others, modeling Your own
love and humility and sacrifice, that they might come to know
and follow You.

May I never again be a slave to my sin but instead be Your devoted
disciple. May I live in Your light, acknowledging the former
darkness in which I was held captive before You rescued me.
I boldly ask these things because of what Christ Jesus has
done for me,
Amen.

Optional Week 9 Activity:

If Jesus' ministry, as described in Luke 4:16-21 included proclaiming good news to the poor, proclaiming freedom for prisoners, recovery of sight for the blind, setting the oppressed free, and proclaiming the year of the Lord's favor, how might you engage in one of those ministry priorities this week?
On a regular basis?

Week Ten—Our Confidence & Encouragement

The word "confidence" has the sense of assurance, certainty, belief, conviction, trust, and faith. It is the opposite of timidity, unbelief, and doubt.

Part of what you are doing in this journey of twelve weeks is to gain confidence by placing your confidence...your trust...your conviction...your belief in God and in what His Word says. You are choosing His Words about you over what you may at times think about yourself, what others may think, or, even more likely what you think they are thinking about you!

His Word says:

> "It is better to take refuge in the Lord than to put confidence in mortals. It is better to take refuge in the Lord than to put confidence in princes."

> "For the Lord will be your confidence and will keep your foot from being caught."

> "In [Christ] and through faith in him we may approach God with freedom and confidence."

> (Psalm 118:8-9; Proverbs 3:26; Ephesians 3:12)

As you grow in your confidence—trust—in the Lord, be encouraged. And, seek to then be an encourager of others.

Week Ten—Our Confidence & Encouragement

Encouragement means to give courage to...to strengthen the heart of...to exhort others—gently pushing them forward toward greater health and maturity.

Scripture is full of commands telling us to be exhorters to one another:

> "Therefore encourage one another with these words."

> "Therefore encourage one another and build up each other, as indeed you are doing."

> "...admonish the idlers, encourage the faint hearted, help the weak, be patient with all of them."

> (1 Thessalonians 4:18; 5:11; 5:14)

Our source of encouragement, again, is God: "May the God of steadfastness and encouragement grant you to live in harmony with one another, in accordance with Christ Jesus" (Romans 15:5). He is the God of encouragement. He enables us to encourage others.

One key way we are encouraged by the Lord is knowing that we are not left to navigate this world on our own with our human abilities and finite resources. Our infinitely wise God gives us His much-needed wisdom. James 1:5 tells us: "If any of you lacks wisdom, you should ask God, who gives generously to all without finding fault, and it will be given to you." We are told that in Christ is "hidden all the treasures of wisdom and knowledge"—available to us so we might "have the full riches of complete understanding" as God encourages and unites us as His people (Colossians 2:2-3). This "wisdom that comes from heaven" is "pure; then peace-loving, considerate, submissive, full of mercy and good fruit, impartial and sincere" (James 3:16-18). And, ultimately, as the Lord guides our hearts, the direction of that guidance is into God's love and Christ's perseverance (2 Thessalonians 3:5).

This week, practice putting your confidence in God and in the words on the following pages—that are the truth about Him and about you.

Day 1
You are completely forgiven. You can know God.

<u>Jeremiah 31:34</u> "...they will all know me, from the least of them to the greatest," declares the Lord. "For I will forgive their wickedness and will remember their sins no more."

<u>2 Corinthians 13:11</u> Finally, brothers and sisters, rejoice! Strive for full restoration, encourage one another, be of one mind, live in peace. And the God of love and peace will be with you.

Day 2
You are saved...completely...through Jesus.

Hebrews 7:24-25 ...because Jesus lives forever, he has a permanent priesthood. Therefore he is able to save completely those who come to God through him, because he always lives to intercede for them.

You can come near to God...with full assurance.

Hebrews 10:21-23 ...and since we have a great priest over the house of God, let us draw near to God with a sincere heart and with the full assurance that faith brings, having our hearts sprinkled to cleanse us from a guilty conscience and having our bodies washed with pure water. Let us hold unswervingly to the hope we profess, for he who promised is faithful.

Day 3
You are anointed and sealed by God.

2 Corinthians 1: 20-22 For no matter how many promises God has made, they are "Yes" in Christ. And so through him the "Amen" is spoken by us to the glory of God. Now it is God who makes both us and you stand firm in Christ. He anointed us, set his seal of ownership on us, and put his Spirit in our hearts as a deposit, guaranteeing what is to come.

Day 4
You have great value to God.

<u>Matthew 6:26</u> Look at the birds of the air; they do not sow or reap or store away in barns, and yet your heavenly Father feeds them. Are you not much more valuable than they?

You are known...completely.

<u>Psalm 139:1-4</u> You have searched me, Lord, and you know me. You know when I sit and when I rise; you perceive my thoughts from afar. You discern my going out and my lying down; you are familiar with all my ways. Before a word is on my tongue you, Lord, know it completely.

Day 5
You are reconciled to God.

<u>Colossians 1:22</u> But now he has reconciled you by Christ's physical body through death to present you holy in his sight, without blemish and free from accusation.

You are never alone...God is always with you.

<u>Psalm 139:7-10</u> Where can I go from your Spirit? Where can I flee from your presence? If I go up to the heavens, you are there; if I make my bed in the depths, you are there. If I rise on the wings of the dawn, if I settle on the far side of the sea, even there your hand will guide me, your right hand will hold me fast.

Day 6
Take a moment now to read these verses aloud.
Insert your name in each blank space. Say it over at least twice.
Savor the thought contained in these words direct from
God to your heart:

In Him YOU (Name)_____ were chosen...YOU were marked
in Him with a seal, the promised Holy Spirit, who is a deposit
guaranteeing our inheritance until the redemption of those who are
God's possession—to the praise of His glory.
Ephesians 1:11-14

In Christ, YOU (Name)_____ bring something unique
to His church, His Body, and each member of His Body belongs
to all the others. You have a different set of gifts, on purpose, by
God's design. Use your gifts faithfully to serve and glorify God
and to encourage others.
Romans 12:5-8

Day 7
Week 10 Prayer:

Lord my Confidence and my Encouragement,
I am so reassured by the fact that I can put my trust and belief
in You and Your Word. You are unfailingly reliable. You are my
Refuge, my Protector, the One who assures me.

Jesus, You are the ultimate Priest and Pastor. You save me
completely and enable me to approach God—as You intercede for
me. You have anointed and sealed me, putting Your Spirit in my
heart. You alone are my guarantee.

I am grateful that You see me as blemishless because of Your work
on the cross and Your victory over death.

Strengthen my heart. Grant me the courage I need. Make me a
healthy exhorter of others. Cause Your church to be a collection of
people who are encouragers. Who build each other up. Who bolster
the faint-hearted. Who aid those who are weak. Who are patient
with everyone. Who live in harmony with one another. Use us in
these holy moments to be a shining example of Your love and unity
to a watching world. Give us a vision for what "full restoration"
looks like. Grant us unity of mind.

I choose to believe today that I am free in Christ, completely
forgiven, known, and never alone. You are always with me—taking
refuge in these truths today,
Amen.

Optional Week 10 Activity:

Read through the entirety of Psalm 139, inserting your own name in place of the pronouns.

Read through Psalm 139 again as a prayer for someone you know—inserting their name in place of the pronouns.

How might you remember the Lord as your source of holy encouragement this week?

Week Eleven—God's Design: Chosen

Chosen. We all want to be picked, to be chosen, selected. We want to be unique, valued, valuable.

Scripture is full of "choosing" language. And, it's all about God choosing you and me. We simply respond to Him reaching out to us. In selecting Israel, God said: "For you are a people holy to the Lord your God; the Lord your God has chosen you out of all the peoples on earth to be His people, His treasured possession" (Deuteronomy 7:6).

Jesus tells us: "I have chosen you out of the world..." (John 15:19).

Paul reminds us: "For we know, brothers and sisters beloved by God, that He has chosen you..." (1 Thessalonians 1:4).

Peter goes on to say: "But you are a chosen people, a royal priesthood, a holy nation, God's special possession, that you may declare the praises of him who called you out of darkness into his wonderful light" (1 Peter 2:9).

You are treasured by God. You ARE chosen. You are God's special possession.

One way to make progress on having a correct view of self in relation to God is to seek to understand His call and His design for you and in relation to the greater Body of Christ. I have had the privilege of teaching classes and doing coaching related to God-given passion and spiritual gifts for over 30 years now. From saturating myself, of necessity, in God's Word about these subjects and preparing to teach it countless times a year, God has helped open my eyes to see a glimpse of His glorious plan—to NOT make me the same as anyone else and to NOT make any of you the same as me or each other—on purpose—because that diversity reflects His glory and accomplishes His will on this planet.

Over time, I've grown to embrace the spiritual gifts He's given me (even the ones I wasn't sure I wanted!), and I can clearly see places where I'm not gifted. I have had many, many experiences where the gifts of others have ministered to me in tangible ways, where I (on my good days) don't compare your gifts with who I'm not, but play to my God-given strengths and applaud yours. I find myself grateful and in awe of those differences.

We tend to feel inadequate when we don't know our gifts, when we don't like the gifts God has given us, or when we are regularly operating outside our areas of giftedness and feeling depleted or frustrated. Make a point of studying gift Scriptures (Romans 12, 1 Corinthians 12, Ephesians 4, 1 Peter 4), taking a free gifts assessment[15], getting familiar with the definitions of spiritual gifts, and using your gifts![16]

Spend time this week believing that you are chosen and uniquely gifted by God to accomplish His purposes in the world.

---

[15] GodGiftsYou.com/Assessment

[16] Access all the resources at GodGiftsYou.com, including the "Gifts-Calling-Purpose" blog (including FAQs about spiritual gifts), the Resources page (including downloadable study guides and gifts definitions), and order the *God. Gifts. You.: Your Unique Calling and Design* six-week workbook to go deeper on the subject of your spiritual gifts.

Day 1
You were uniquely formed by God.

Isaiah 44:2 This is what the Lord says—he who made you, who formed you in the womb, and who will help you: Do not be afraid.

You are chosen...to be holy. You have received God's grace in Jesus.

Ephesians 1:4-6 For he chose us in him before the creation of the world to be holy and blameless in his sight. In love he predestined us for adoption to sonship through Jesus Christ, in accordance with his pleasure and will—to the praise of his glorious grace, which he has freely given us in the One he loves.

Day 2
You were bought at a price.

<u>1 Corinthians 6:19-20</u> Do you not know that your bodies are temples of the Holy Spirit, who is in you, whom you have received from God? You are not your own; you were bought at a price. Therefore honor God with your bodies.

Day 3
You are differently-gifted by God on purpose.

<u>1 Corinthians 12:4-6</u> There are different kinds of gifts, but the same Spirit distributes them. There are different kinds of service, but the same Lord. There are different kinds of working, but in all of them and in everyone it is the same God at work.

You are called and gifted…for always.

<u>Romans 11:29</u> …for God's gifts and his call are irrevocable.

Day 4
You have unique gifts...given by God...for you to use...for the benefit of all.

<u>1 Corinthians 12:7, 11</u> Now to each one the manifestation of the Spirit is given for the common good...All these are the work of one and the same Spirit, and he distributes them to each one, just as he determines.

You are a unique part of the church—the Body of Christ.

<u>Romans 12:4-6a</u> For just as each of us has one body with many members, and these members do not all have the same function, so in Christ we, though many, form one body, and each member belongs to all the others. We have different gifts, according to the grace given to each of us.

Day 5
Your contribution is not in vain.

<u>1 Corinthians 15:58</u> Therefore, my dear brothers and sisters, stand firm. Let nothing move you. Always give yourselves fully to the work of the Lord, because you know that your labor in the Lord is not in vain.

Day 6

Take a moment now to read these verses aloud.
Insert your name in each blank space. Say it over at least twice.
Savor the thought contained in these words direct from
God to your heart:

The One Who calls YOU, (Name)_____ is faithful,
and He will do it.
1 Thessalonians 5:24

If YOU (Name)_____ are faithless, He remains faithful…
2 Timothy 2:13

I, the Lord, have loved YOU (Name) _____ with
an everlasting love; I have drawn YOU (Name) _____ with
unfailing kindness.
Jeremiah 31:3

Day 7
Week 11 Prayer:

Lord of my unique design,
I am humbled by the fact that You love me and create me and
choose me and set me apart for Your purposes. I am amazed that
You provide for me by placing me just where You want me in Your
Body, the Church.

Help me to see and understand Your call and my unique design.
Reveal to me the passions that You have given to motivate me to
make commitments. Show me the spiritual gifts with which You
have empowered and equipped me to be effective for You and for
the greater good.

I sit in wonder at Your design for uniqueness and diversity in the
human race—that I am not like any other person who has come
before me or will come after me. I praise You that this variety is a
reflection of Your glory and Your plan to reach all nations.

Thank You that I do not have all of the gifts—that no one does.
Your intent was for us to rely on one another in beautiful variety
and holy unity while each of us reflects different aspects of
Your character. I am grateful today for those in my life who are
differently gifted—who show me what the areas of my non-gifts
look like when empowered by Your Spirit. I pause now to name
these people and their gifts aloud to You. [PAUSE and name
people who have gifts different from yours.]

I choose today to embrace the spiritual gifts You have given me,
to commit to developing and using them, and to recognize and call
out the gifts in others around me. I will be fully satisfied with You
and Your provision for my life. I will sing praises to You today.
[PAUSE and worship the Lord aloud in song.]

I pray all these things trusting in Your faithfulness,
Amen.

Optional Week 11 Activity:
Take the free spiritual gifts assessment at
GodGiftsYou.com/Assessment.

Click on the link in your results and read the
definitions of each gift.

Memorize the list of your top 3-5 spiritual gifts.

Ask the Lord how and where you are to use them in the coming
days and weeks.

Seek ways to encourage and affirm the gifts you see in others.

Week Twelve—God's Compassion: Gratitude & Satisfaction

Gratitude. Thankfulness. Appreciation. Gratefulness.

One way we can practice adopting the right perspective about Our Heavenly Father and about ourselves is to practice being grateful. For the big things. For the small things. For the medium-sized things. Remember the Philippians 4 passage where Paul says he had learned contentment? He begins that section of verses with "Rejoice in the Lord always" and "In every situation, by prayer and petition, with thanksgiving, present your requests to God" (Philippians 4:4-8). Somehow, Paul's ability to learn to be content was linked to his CHOICE to rejoice—not necessarily in his circumstances but in the Lord. It was connected to his constant prayer and petition to God—expressing his needs, his frustrations, his unbelief—but always WITH thanksgiving.

If finding our satisfaction in God and being at peace with ourselves and others comes from having a new perspective, one way to refocus our vision in the right place is to practice being thankful. It's a way to exercise our "trust-muscles"—a way to say to God that we are choosing to lean on Him—to lean into Him even when things don't always make sense.

The Lord is the One who renews your mind and heart. The Lord is the One Who shows You His perfect will. Each time you offer yourself to the Lord in service, He considers that WORSHIP! (See Romans 12:1-2.)

Week Twelve—God's Compassion: Gratitude & Satisfaction

For these twelve weeks, you have immersed yourself in God's Word—a place you cannot go wrong. His Word continually instructs us:

> "He will instruct them in the ways they should choose."

> "Choose my instruction instead of silver, knowledge rather than choice gold."

> "Lord, Your law is written within my heart."

> (Psalm 40:8; 25:12; Proverbs 8:10)

Keep returning to Scripture to learn more and more of what He says to you and of you. Letting the Bible define who the Lord is is powerful. The more you seek Him the more you will know and trust Him. He actively loves and cares for you: "Yet the Lord longs to be gracious to you; therefore He will rise up to show you compassion. For the Lord is a God of justice. Blessed are all who wait for Him!" (Isaiah 30:18)

The Gospels are full of examples of Jesus' love for sinners like you and me. "When He saw the crowds, He had compassion on them, because they were harassed and helpless…" and "When Jesus landed and saw a large crowd, He had compassion on them and healed their sick" (Matthew 9:36; 14:14).

Do you feel harassed and helpless? God's compassion and love for you have no limits.

This week, choose to be grateful that God is good. His love endures. Forever. And ever. And ever. Amen.

Day 1
You can live in Jesus' love for you—a wide, long, high, and deep love.

Ephesians 3:17-19 And I pray that you, being rooted and established in love, may have power, together with all the Lord's holy people, to grasp how wide and long and high and deep is the love of Christ, and to know this love that surpasses knowledge—that you may be filled to the measure of all the fullness of God.

Day 2
**You can know the Lord's unfailing, never-ending love
and full restoration.**

Psalm 130:7 ...put your hope in the Lord, for with the Lord is
unfailing love and with him is full redemption.

Psalm 89:33 ...I will not take My love from him[her], nor will I
ever betray My faithfulness.

Day 3
You are blessed with every spiritual blessing in Christ.

Ephesians 1:3 Praise be to the God and Father of our Lord Jesus
Christ, who has blessed us in the heavenly realms with every
spiritual blessing in Christ.

You can be fully satisfied in God.

Psalm 63:4-6 I will praise you as long as I live, and in your name I
will lift up my hands. I will be fully satisfied as with the richest of
foods; with singing lips my mouth will praise you.

Day 4
You have the power of God at work in you.

<u>Ephesians 3:20-21</u> Now to him who is able to do immeasurably more than all we ask or imagine, according to his power that is at work within us, to him be glory in the church and in Christ Jesus throughout all generations, for ever and ever! Amen.

Day 5
You are entrusted with God's message of reconciliation.

2 Corinthians 5:18-19 All this is from God, who reconciled us to himself through Christ and gave us the ministry of reconciliation: that God was reconciling the world to himself in Christ, not counting people's sins against them. And he has committed to us the message of reconciliation.

Day 6
Take a moment now to read the following verses aloud.
Insert your name in each blank space. Say it over at least twice.
Savor the thought contained in these words direct from
God to your heart:

Lord, root and establish ME in your love. Gift ME your power,
together with all your holy people, to grasp how wide and long
and high and deep is the love of Christ, and to know this love that
surpasses knowledge—that I may be filled to the measure
of all the fullness of God.
Ephesians 3:17-19

He [the Lord] sends from heaven and saves YOU (Name)_____,
rebuking those who hotly pursue YOU—God sends forth His love
and His faithfulness to YOU (Name)_____.
Psalm 57:3

Day 7
Week 12 Prayer:

Generous Lord,
I am grateful to You. Thankful for who You are. I choose today to
stop and appreciate the large and small things You have done in
my life and the lives of those around me. [PAUSE to detail these
things—try to list at least 10.]

I decide, with Paul, to rejoice in You always. I commit—"in every
situation"—"by prayer and petition"—"with thanksgiving"—to
present my requests to You. No matter my circumstances, I will be
a person of prayer and rejoicing.

Help me to find my satisfaction in You, to be at peace with myself
and with others. Give me Your perspective, especially in this
increasingly fraught world of strife. I promise to lean on You and
lean into You even when my situation doesn't make sense.

Make me a minister and messenger of Your reconciliation. Saturate
me in the story of my own holy reunion with You through Jesus.

I say aloud that You are good. You offer "full redemption." I put
my hope in You. Your love endures. You are the same yesterday,
today, and forever.
Amen.

Optional Week 12 Activity:

Meditate on "Yet the Lord longs to be gracious to you; therefore He will rise up to show you compassion. For the Lord is a God of justice. Blessed are all who wait for Him!" (Isaiah 30:18). Receive the Lord's great compassion today.

Spend some time today being grateful. List at least five things. Bring those to the Lord in praise and gratitude. Consider doing this as a daily practice.

How might you practice prayer and petition with thanks?

Going Forward

As you continue to refocus your mind and heart, with the Spirit's help, on Jesus, I hope that you have a corresponding increasingly new and refreshing perspective on yourself in relation to Him. Scripture says again and again that complete contentment and peace is found only in God (not in things, not in activity, not in service for God, not even in what God provides for us): "...when I awake, I will be satisfied with seeing your likeness, [Lord]. I will be fully satisfied as with the richest of foods; with singing lips my mouth will praise you...earth has nothing I desire besides you" (Psalm 17:15; 63:5; 73:25).

The promises you have meditated on these past twelve weeks are always current. God promises to always love us, and to always be with us: "Never will I leave you; never will I forsake you" (Hebrews 13:5). Jesus bought us peace with His death...a peace with God through Jesus. And Jesus left His disciples with the promise of peace—peace IN HIM in spite of the world's troubles. "I have told you these things, so that in Me you may have peace. In this world you will have trouble. But take heart! I have overcome the world" (John 16:33).

You can be healed of that sense of discontent and "un-chosenness" by the God of the universe who created you on purpose and who loves you as much as you can possibly be loved! "The Lord longs to be gracious to you; therefore He will rise up to show you compassion..." (Psalm 51:1). May you always remember that God is "compassionate and gracious, slow to anger, abounding in love and faithfulness" (Psalm 86:15). May He give you the ability to believe that with all your heart!

God's LOVE is primary. You are BELOVED before you do or say anything. Let's continue to ABIDE in Jesus and His unfailing LOVE for us, taking time now to pray to those ends.

> *God our Great Father...we sit in wonder at Your love that reaches to the heavens...Your faithfulness that stretches to the skies. Your Word reminds us that your everlasting love is priceless, unfailing, and trustworthy. Today, we thank you for this great, unreserved love that You have so generously and undeservedly lavished on us. We are so grateful that You call us Your children. We delight in being called Your masterpiece...so intentionally knit together by You—each of us unrepeatable miracles with great purpose—to glorify You. You call us chosen, holy, special to You.*
>
> *We are also thankful that You are the One who is continuously redeeming and transforming us into Jesus' likeness. You are not content to leave us floundering...but You desire that we become the best version of who You created us to be. You have called us out of darkness and into the stunning light of Your Presence. We choose to believe what You say about us...and we ask that You erase the lies the enemy has tried to plant and the falsehoods that our culture fans into flame and destroy the thoughts that drag us down.*
>
> *Faithful Lord, help each of us believe deep in our souls that You love us. Encourage and strengthen our hearts and minds—to abide with You...to receive Your love. Help us to love ourselves so that we let Your love pass through us to others...that they might know they are loved.*
>
> *This week, remind us of the Holy Spirit's power within each of us...and of Your wide, long, high, and deep love for us. Fill us with Your joy and Your fullness. Help us submit to You—to what You want for each of us—as we live flourishing lives overflowing with Your Living Water.*
> *AMEN*

Reflect back on the past twelve weeks. What has stayed with you? What is stirring? How will you incorporate these lessons into your life?

About the Author

Shirley Giles Davis, author of the *God. Gifts. You. Your Unique Calling and Design* workbook, *Your Unique Design Class Guide, Your Unique Design Facilitator Guide, DIOS. DONES. TÚ.: Tu llamado y diseño único* (Spanish Edition), and the "Gifts-Calling-Purpose" blog, is a consultant, coach, and facilitator who has worked with hundreds of faith-based organizations, nonprofit agencies, and executive leaders in a diversity of fields for four decades. Shirley is passionate about helping individuals and teams become their very best. She is in her 27th year on staff as Catalyst for Equipping at her church.

Books and Resources

• Take this free spiritual gifts assessment: **https://godgiftsyou. com/assessment** or this free Spanish language spiritual gifts assessment: **https://ggy-spanish-da8b2a8fd895.herokuapp. com/**

• The *God. Gifts. You.: Your Unique Calling and Design* workbook by Shirley Giles Davis is a six-week deep dive into your calling, purpose, gifts, and design. Excellent for individuals, groups, or your entire church. The Spanish version: *DIOS. DONES. TÚ.: Tu llamado y diseño único* is also available.

• The *Your Unique Design Class Guide* and *Your Unique Design Facilitator Guide* together can help your church or group learn more about gifts-based life and ministry.

• The above-mentioned books are all currently available on Amazon.com.

• Downloadable Resources—at GodGiftsYou.com—See:
  • "Sample List of Interest Areas"
  • "Your Spiritual Gifts—A Study Guide"
  • "Knowing Your Unique Calling and Purpose Study Guide"
  • "Whole-Life Ministry: A Form of Worship"
  • "Grace-Giving"
  • "Living into Your Calling"